IMPORT/EXPORT GUIDE HOW TO GET FOREIGN BUYERS AND EXPORT YOUR PRODUCTS WORLDWIDE

IMPORT/EXPORT
GUIDE
HOW TO GET FOREIGN BUYERS AND EXPORT YOUR PRODUCTS WORLDWIDE

Included: 50 Global e-marketplaces to get International Buyers from over 165 countries.

Solomon Ternder

LEGAL NOTES

IMPORT/EXPORT: HOW TO GET FOREIGN CONTACTS AND EXPORT YOUR PRODUCTS WORLDWIDE

www.solomonternder.com

For permissions contact:

solomonternder@gmail.com

Disclaimer

This book has been prepared as a general informational guide. The information contained herein is not intended to provide legal advice or substitute for information otherwise available from relevant government agencies, institutions and departments. While every effort has been made to verify the accuracy of the information at the time of writing, the author bears no legal responsibility or otherwise for the accuracy or content, as information is dynamic and subject to change.

DEDICATION

This book is dedicated to the Almighty God and to my lovely family.

FOREWORD

"Success doesn't just come and find you, you have to go out and get it." KushandWizdom

Nowadays, the use of internet has become a normal day to day activity in the world. It provided the world with so much information thus making it easier and faster for individuals to communicate and attain information worldwide. It greatly helped many businesses gain larger markets, patrons and create services that easily reach out costumers. It provided avenue to circulate information in regard to the product or services that reaches out to millions of people across the globe.

As a Researcher who is always beating a deadline, meeting Mr. Solomon Ternder is a great blessing. His book on Moringa Oleifera, alleviates my pain of going through lots of complicated information for my feasibility studies. The clarity and comprehensiveness of his books unloaded my burdens. And I am taking this opportunity to thank him for opening the door for a greater success in my endeavors.

This new book about Import and Export Guide deserves a place at the top of your "must read" list. It's a great pleasure for me to recommend this book. This book is filled with a practical guide portraying all the guidelines and tools you need to start an import and export business. I hope it will lead to a rewarding career for you, and I wish you every success in your ventures to a more profitable business.

Vicky "Leyann" Veso
Researcher
Manila, Philippines

ACKNOWLEDGMENT

I would like to sincerely appreciate God for the opportunity to start and finish this project. I specially acknowledge my wife, **OluwaDamilola**, who has been a huge support and allowing me the space to work on the manuscript. **Redeemed** and **Joseph**, you guys rock! I give it to you.

I would like to acknowledge Pastor Daniel Okpara who has tremendously shaped my skills. To the entire KDP/CREATESPACE group members, I owe you lots of love. Your input has made this work come out well.

I must appreciate my cover Designer, Mr. Martins, for doing a great work and giving the advice I needed to make this look professional. God bless.

WHY I WROTE THIS BOOK

Beloved, I wrote this book in response to calls and emails I have received **from different people asking for information on how to get exportation leads** for their import/export business, particularly those involved in Agro products like **Moringa oleifera**, **cashew nuts**, **sesame seeds,** etc. This is therefore an answer to many requests and I believe you will find great value from the following pages.

With this resource, you are empowered to get foreign contacts and succeed in your exportation business **whether you are just starting out** or you have been involved in the business for a long time.

To contact me fast, you may shoot a mail to **solomonternder@gmail.com**

See you on the other side of Export business.

Blessings!

TABLE OF CONTENTS

INTRODUCTION

Thanks for buying this book. I am sure your heart's desire is to get foreign buyers for your export business. The truth is, that is a very important aspect of your business that cannot be overemphasized. So I want to congratulate you for buying this book. Definitely, you have got the best solution to your **export leads generation challenge**. Now you have in your hands a tool which will enable you get foreign buyers like a Ninja.

It has been the desire of many businesses to expand to the shores of other countries but one of the challenges has always been how to get customers in other countries. Similarly, every established **Exporter needs more export leads to continue in business**. Whether you are just starting out in export business or you have been involved in export business for a long time, I know your desire is to get more foreign clients to sell to.

Finding Export leads is therefore essential to the success of any export business. In this book, we have solved the problem for you. We have researched and compiled the easiest ways to get export leads by yourself on the internet in the comfort of your bedroom!

Here, at last you have the solution to your greatest marketing challenge. Now you can easily locate the foreign buyers you have always desired so as to do more business internationally.

Therefore take time to go through this book and follow the links to the several **business to business (B2B)** or **business to customer** (B2C) portals and/or e-marketplaces where you will get the leads as explained.

You will need to be connected to the internet as you read the book since most of the content is to be done practically online. This is a practically oriented book; you will be doing hands-on application online as your read. It is quite a fun and interactive way to find export leads.

CHAPTER ONE

START YOUR JOURNEY OF FINDING EXPORT LEADS

Beloved, like I stated earlier, the focus of this book is to teach you...

...*the* ***easiest strategies to getting foreign clients*** *from any part of the world for your exportation business online.*

Exportation cuts across many industries including **jewelry**, **cosmetics**, **textile**, **pharmaceutical**, **petroleum, automobile, oil and gas,** etc.

It is the desire of every Exporter or any other player in export commodities supply chain to have a market for their products. Many products have more value in other parts of the world where they are not found.

Farmers, for instance, always look for ways to export their agro products for foreign exchange.

Meanwhile, there are people who are looking for those who will supply them the following products: **herbs**, **spices**, **moringa**, **sesame seeds**, **leather**, **charcoal**, **sunflower seeds**, **organic chemicals**, **pharmaceuticals**, **Black pepper**, **Refined Sunflower Oils**, **Gem stones**, **Charcoal**, **Red chili pepper**, **Sunflower Oil**, **Copper**, **Lime Stone** and many other products everywhere on business to business(B2B) e-marketplaces and portals, Facebook agro business groups, LinkedIn agro business groups online business forums, etc.

As a **Digital Marketing Consultant**, I have carefully researched and put together this resource to help just anyone trying to find export leads for their agro products and other exportable products.

The following steps are what I suggest you start with:

1. JOIN RELEVANT GROUPS ON FACEBOOK AND LINKEDIN

Join www.Facebook.com and www.linkedin.com and search for relevant groups and pages to join and like respectively. Simply join the groups and once approved, you can post your products for sale and get potential international buyers. **Facebook allows you to join up to 6000 groups**. Your duty is to search for the groups that are relevant to your business and join. After joining the groups, you can now begin the search for export leads. Make sure the groups contain members from many different parts of the world. For instance, to get buyers of moringa seeds on Facebook groups easily, simply click the **search field** which is located at the **top right** side of the group page and type "sesame buyers".

You may **save the search** too so that any further posts about sesame buyers in the group will automatically be sent to you by Facebook as an alert. When you do this search, you will find a number of people looking for bulk sesame seeds to buy.

Learn how to join Facebook groups here.

Learn how to join LinkedIn groups here.

Also, you may join **IMPORT/EXPORT** groups on the above social networks and relate with people from other countries. This way, you will eventually find business leads. This is known as **relational marketing**.

> NOTE: ***I only use moringa here as an example. You may type leather, cocoa, charcoal, textile <u>or any other specific export product</u> you are dealing with.***

You may contact such prospective buyers to transact with and who knows, if all goes well, you might be exporting sesame seeds to China and making steady income. That is if you have the bulk sesame seeds to sell in this case. You would have to engage the services of a good freight forwarder to enable you facilitate the export business. Please always seek the advice from professional freight forwarders you can trust. Read on to learn how to get freight forwarders to work with.

2. SETUP A FACEBOOK GLOBAL PAGE

Facebook has an amazing feature which enables you to set up mobile-ready business Pages and advertising solutions to help you reach people in every country and on every device. "**We're building tools to help you**

more easily connect with customers, no matter where they are." according to Facebook. Learn more about the Facebook Global Page here; Go here to set it up on Facebook now.

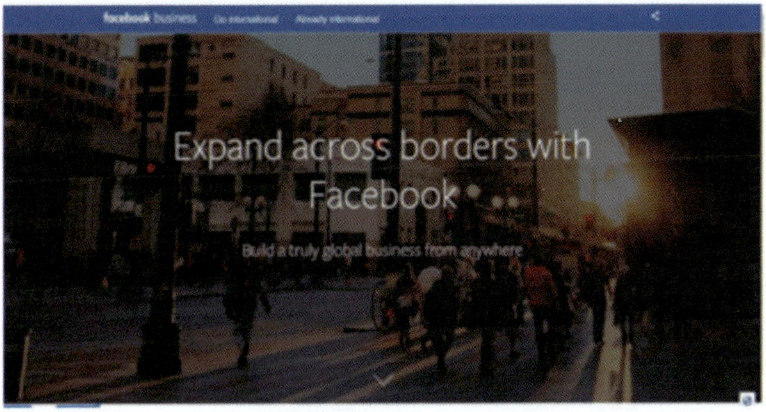

3. REGISTER ON IMPORT/EXPORT E-MARKETPLACES

I export MORINGA seeds to China. You can learn from my own experience. In my own case, I registered on Alibaba. You can register on http://www.alibaba.com as ***a seller*** and get leads for agro and other commodities export. That is one way you could get leads. If you pay to become a premium member on **ALIBABA**, you may be literally bombarded by buyers of the **specific export product**! I will deal more on that later.

4. START A BLOG/WEBSITE

Start a blog like www.moringawealthandhealth.com and write promotional and educational **search engine optimized** articles about your export products. If you do that, you can also have people visit the blog from search engines like **Google** and contact you for sales. You must ensure to put your contact details on your blog/website in the **Contact Us** page to enable prospective buyers contact you.

Most of the leads we get come from our blog!

If you are not able to setup a blog by yourself, you can outsource on freelancing websites like http://www.fiverr.com or **contact us for a blog set-up service.**

5. BUY BUYERS LEADS(CONTACTS)

You may buy export leads from certain B2B market places if you need contacts list REAL **FAST!** Therefore continue reading to learn how to do it yourself.

But if you are in a hurry, contact us now for leads. See the email address above. Note that we would **NOT** give you the leads for free! So do not mail or call to ask for free export leads of your export products... Lol!

STRATEGIES FOR GETTING ONLINE/OFFLINE EXPORT LEADS

Finding foreign (i.e. international) buyers is one of the major tasks for any **export oriented business**. Therefore, every export business must have a concrete strategy to find foreign buyers. Your strategy must include **online** as well as **offline** Promotions.

A Powerful strategy for How to find Foreign Buyers / Overseas Buyers online and offline include (but not limited to) the following activities:

- **Endeavour to build a professional blog/website**

You have to design a mobile responsive, multilingual and international **blog/website**. The blog/website should flaunt your **products portfolio**, **certifications, testimonials**, etc. Since the website is your first impression in front of a visiting prospective buyer, make sure it looks professional. See an example below: http://www.parvenuventureslimited.com/home/

- **Endeavour to attend Trade Shows**

Endeavour to attend various **international trade fairs**. Build up relationships and do follow up communications to enable you get export orders eventually.

Kindly visit this site for trade shows news and events http://www.tsnn.com

- **Check Import- Export Trade Data**

It is highly advisable to use available import export data base to find **importers' list** and **countries** that need products from your country which you have interest in exporting. You can find such data online and offline from your country export promotion council.

- **Social Media Marketing**

Nowadays, the world has become a global village. So you can leverage on social media to increase your business reach and visibility. Create business accounts and pages on major social network platforms like **LinkedIn**, **Facebook**, **Instagram**, **Twitter**, etc. Interact in Groups where people 'gather' to make discussions around your business niche. That way, you can connect with potential International buyers of your products.

- **Export Promotion Council and Foreign Embassies**

Endeavour to stay connected with your respective country **export promotion council** (EPC). Also stay connected with various foreign embassies to enable you get importers' details. Almost every country has such export promotion councils. Their activities include helping exporters get exports leads, among others. They may also extend their services in finding buyers for your product or give you useful information to help.

- **Foreign Agents**

You can appoint an agent in the foreign countries who will find buyers on your behalf. For instance you live in the United States and intend to export your goods to Ghana. You may now check to see companies in Ghana that can be your agents there. The agents will now facilitate your export business in Ghana. It is wise to deal with corporate businesses registered with the appropriate authorities rather than individuals.

CHAPTER TWO

HOW TO REGISTER A FREE ACCOUNT ON B2B E-MARKETPLACES.

I will take you by hand now and teach you how to register on selected B2B export e-marketplaces. Some of the e-marketplaces are absolutely FREE with no form of payment at all. Others offer a limited FREE account and **PREMIUM** accounts **for a fee** which is renewed **periodically** (monthly, yearly, etc). You may choose the free options to start with before eventually upgrading to the premium options.

HOW TO REGISTER AND GET BUYERS ON INDIA MART

Kindly do this online using your computer and internet connection so you can understand fully. It is not meant to be read alone but done practically.

www.indiamart.com

India Mart is currently India's largest B2B marketplace that facilitates the connection of exporters and importers from different parts of the world. According to statistics, Indiamart gets more than 1.6 million daily visits and around 9 million page views per day.

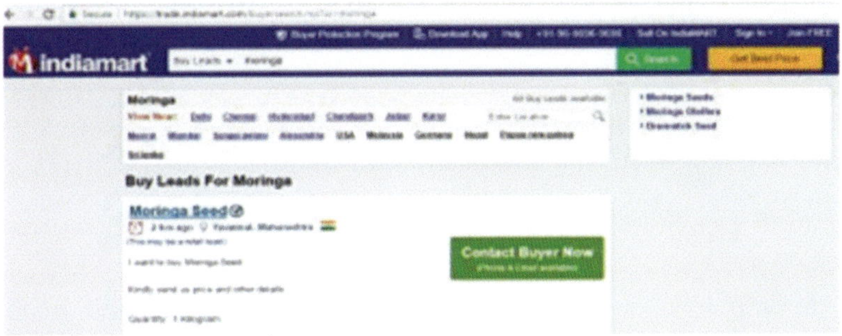

1. Visit www.indiamart.com
2. Click Join
3. Enter your email address

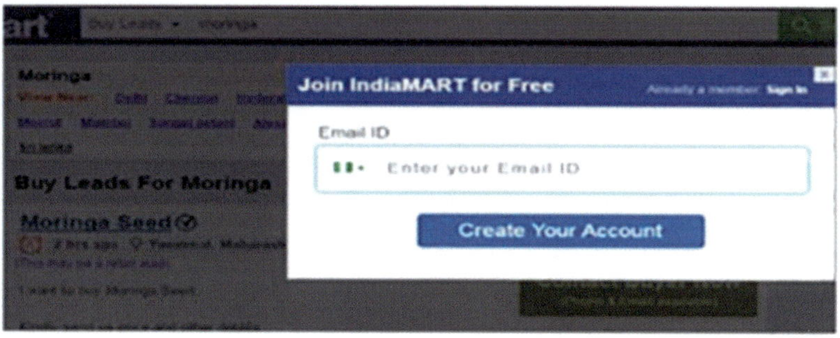

4. Enter your name, city and mobile

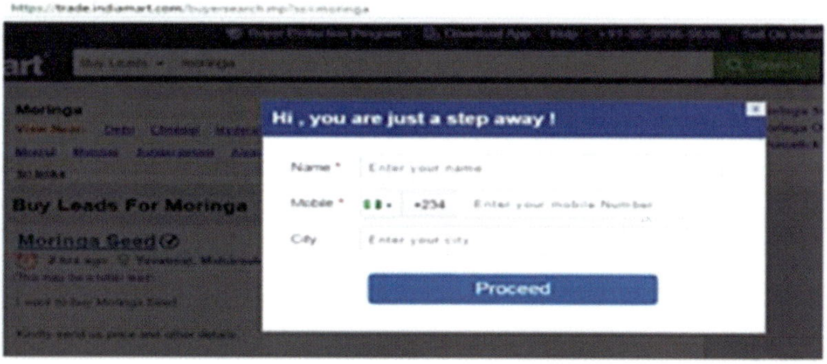

5. Verify email address.

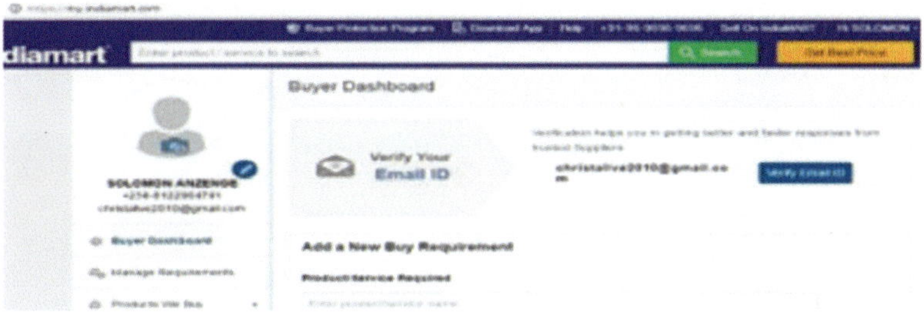

Now that you are registered, you can post an item for sale.

HOW TO POST AN ITEM FOR SALE

1. Click SALE ON INDIAMART as shown below:

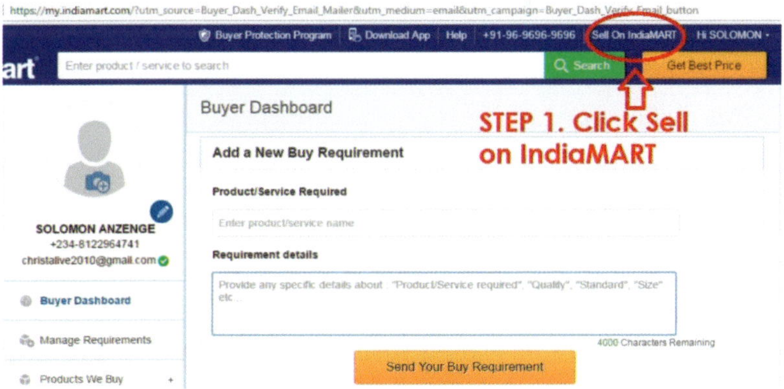

2. Click Continue.

You will be redirected to register as a SELLER this time around.

3. Enter your business details as shown below:

Under "BUSINESS TYPE" Choose ***EXPORTER***

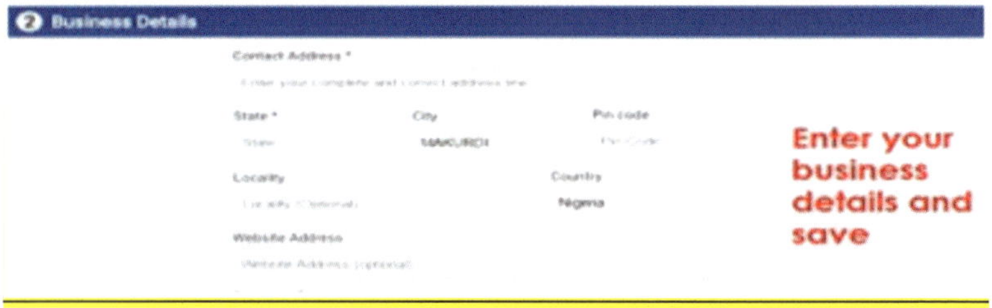

4. Enter Product details and SAVE:

In this case, **Moringa seeds**, moringa leaf powder, moringa oil, **cashew nuts, sesame seeds**, gall stones, laptop, jewelry, phones, wood, diapers, chocolate, clothing, books, bags, cars, foot wears, glasses, creams, soaps, toiletries, mirror, etc. depending on which product you want to sell. You have the opportunity to register four products.

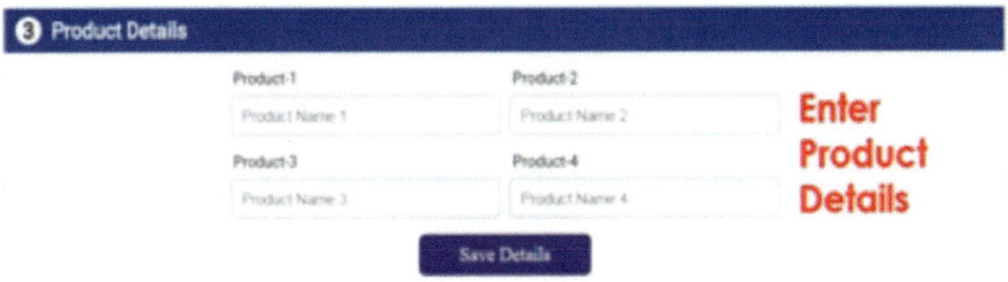

5. On the next page, you will see this message: ***"Business Profile of your company is incomplete, please update Fact Sheet"***

Click update Fact Sheet to be directed to where you will add more details to your profile. See picture below:

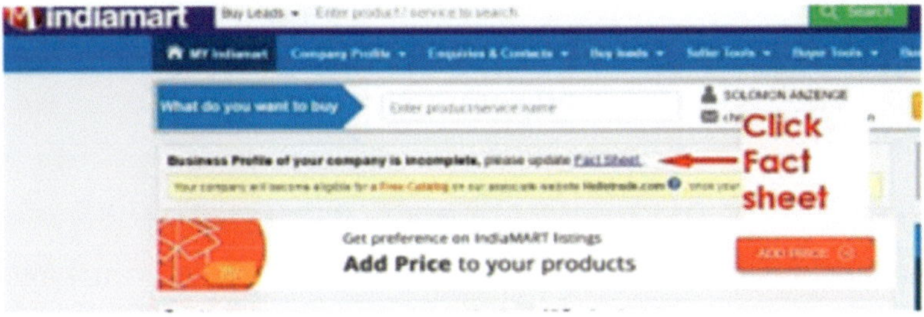

6. Provide your business statutory details as shown below:

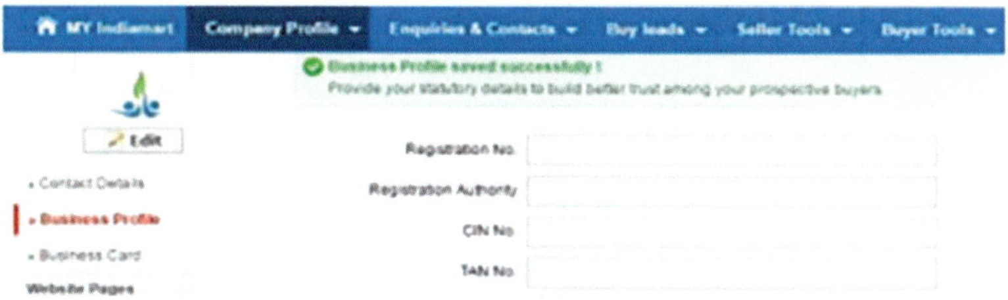

After providing your details, you may be added to the SELLERS DATABASE.

STEPS ON HOW TO GET INTERNATIONAL BUYERS ON INDIAMART

1. Navigate to SELL ON INDIAMART on the top right corner of the website.

2. In the **BUY LEADS** field, type the product you want to sell and click **SEARCH**. Example: moringa seeds. See picture below.

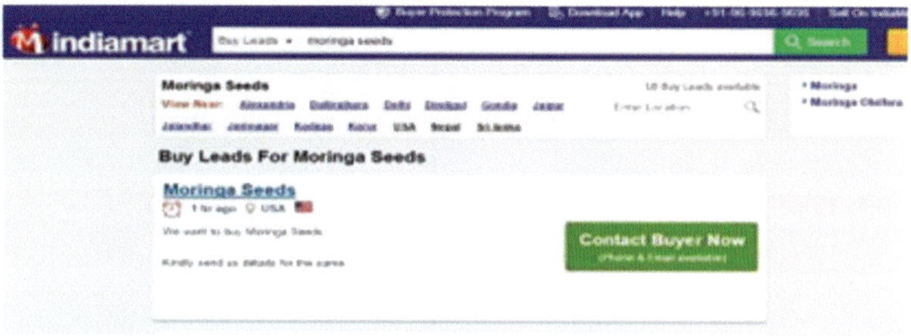

You will then see different buyers listed.

3. Contact Buyers.

Simply click on the "**Contact Buyer Now**" button to show their contact details.

4. Indiamart will give you options to pay for only **1 LEAD, 25 LEADS or 50 LEADS** as the case may be.

Note that they are selling the leads.

At the time of compiling this report,

1 LEAD = 449 RUPEES (equivalent to $7)

25 LEADS =5,000 RUPEES (equivalent to $77)

50 LEADS = 10,000 RUPEES (equivalent to $1550)

You will then be re-directed to the payment page as shown below:

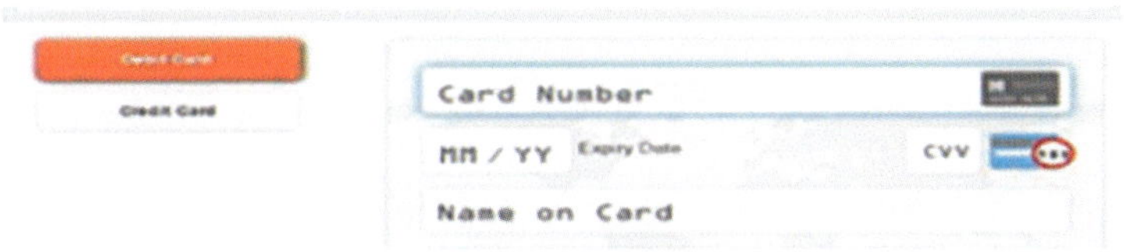

5. Enter your card details (Choose the appropriate card type: DEBIT/CREDIT card) and click pay now.

Now you have access to the number of buyers you paid for.

Please note that if you paid for 25 or 50 LEADS, you can:

- **View thousands of Buy Leads, but pay only for the ones you choose.**
- **Make your own customer contact list.**

Look at the picture below to see

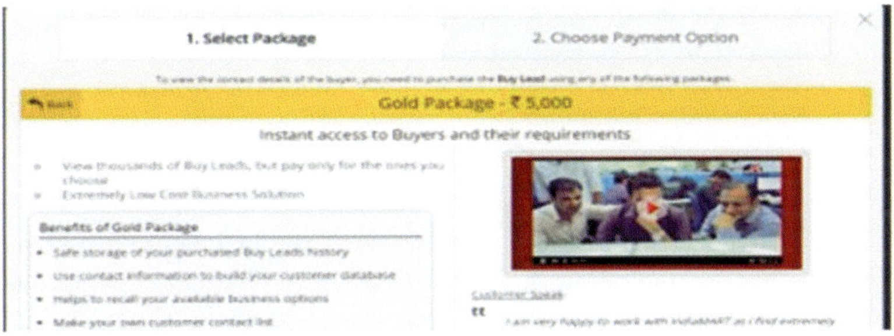

HOW TO REGISTER AND GET BUYERS ON GO 4 WORLD BUSINESS

https://www.go4worldbusiness.com

1. Visit https://www.go4worldbusiness.com and click beside login, choose "NOT A MEMBER? FREE SIGN UP"

2. Fill the form and submit. You will be sent a registration confirmation mail. Check your mail and click the link sent to **confirm registration** appropriately.

3. Sign in to your account and enter the commodity you want to sell at the **SEARCH FIELD**, and then hit the **FIND BUYERS** button as shown below:

4. Browse through the available Buyers list and contact any of your choice (by clicking **INQUIRE NOW**) for business. See example below.

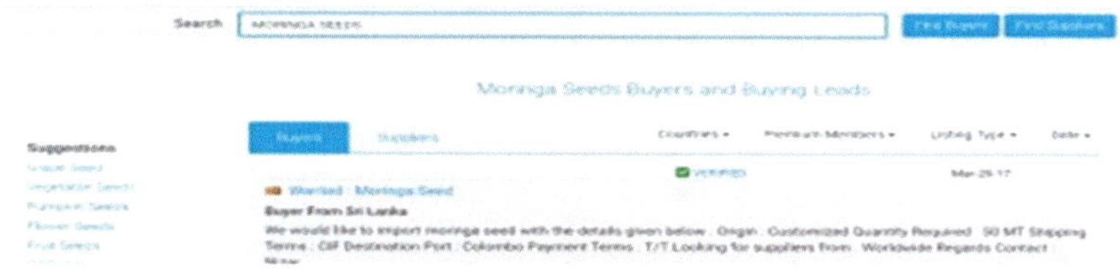

5. Enter the enquiry details including **MINIMUM ORDER QUANTITY**, **PRICING**, etc as shown below: Then click **INQUIRE NOW** at the bottom.

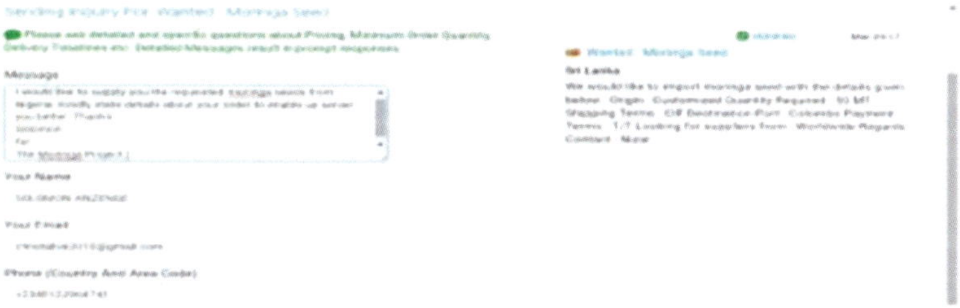

After you have registered, **GO4WORLDBUSINESS** will give you one **ENQUIRY** to buyers per week as a FREE MEMBER.

See example below

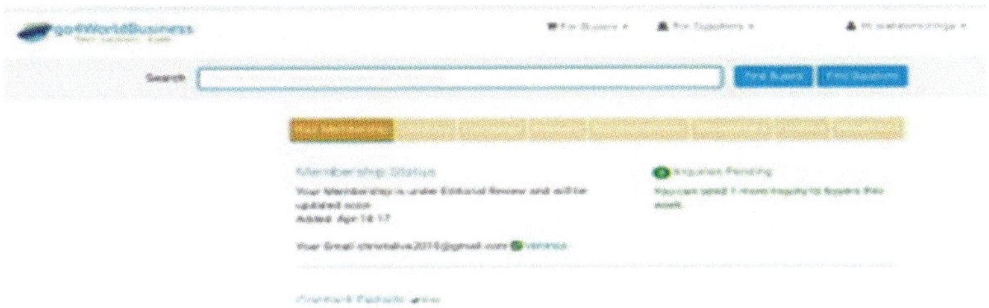

Now you can follow the instructions as shown above for **Indiamart** and **GO4WORLDBUSINESS** to register in the portals and e-market places below. Kindly follow the methods discussed above to get buyers. Please note that each portal/e-market place **may vary** in their website layout hence slightly different approaches have to be applied to register and find buyers as the case may be.

CHAPTER THREE

LIST OF B2B E-MARKETPLACES FOR GETTING EXPORT LEADS ONLINE

Global Trade dot net.

http://www.globaltrade.net

GlobalTrade (dot) net is a service that offers a great deal of importers and exporters the first online directory of **Global Trade Service Providers**. In this directory, importers and exporters can find over 60,000 service providers that can assist them in their international trade transactions.

On this platform, you can find Freight Forwarders too apart from export leads. Global Trade has made it a one stop shop for you. So go through through the website

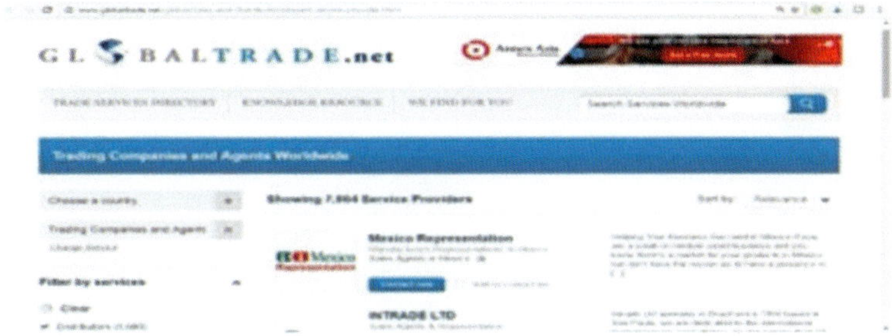

Trade Zone

http://www.tradezone.com

Tradezone.com is one of the global trade centers designed for suppliers, manufacturers, exporters, import export businesses and business opportunity seekers.

It is absolutely100% free to use. But before you register, read the how it works section of the website.

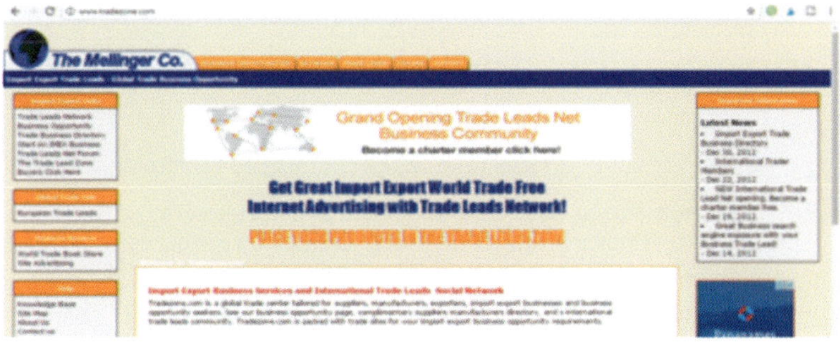

Many exporters are profiled on the website.

For instance, I found this African company exporting sesame seeds on Trade Zone. See his page below

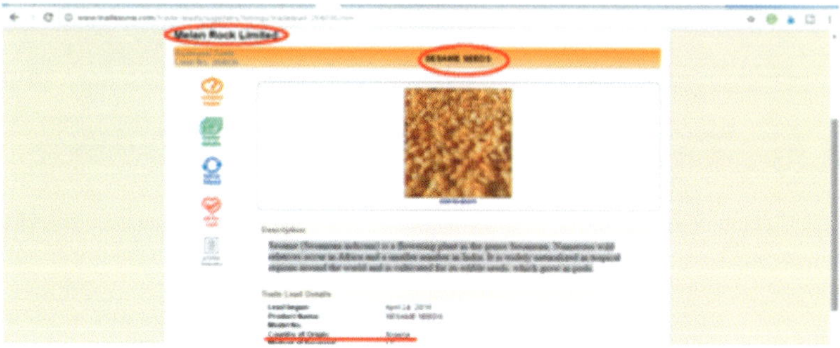

Go4worldbusiness

https://www.go4worldbusiness.com/

Headquartered in the US, Go4worldbusiness, since 1997, for the last 20 years, they have been working with companies, small and large, to grow their business worldwide.

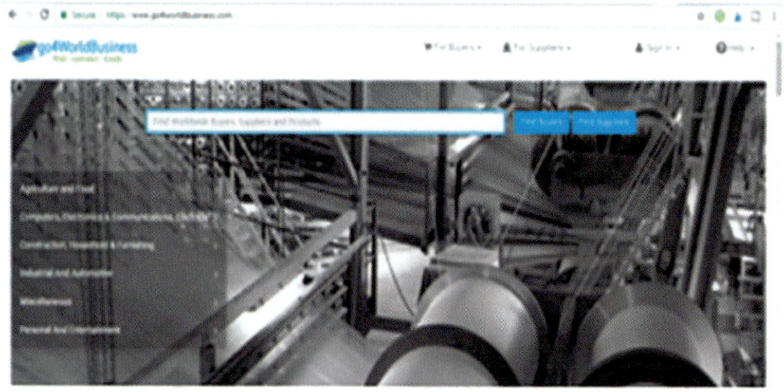

FOREIGN-TRADE ONLINE

http://www.foreign-trade.com/

How to register and profile your business on foreign trade dot com.

According to Foreign Trade Online, there are many opportunities to promote and market your products or services on their website.

Simply follow the steps below:

1. To start with, simply register and introduce your company to the global trade community.
2. After registration, your company can participate in the largest international B2B community. Then po-

tential customers can now easily find the products and services that you have listed.

3. Add all your products and services and start promoting and marketing them to the world all year round
4. You may create and manage sub-accounts for sales representatives in your company.
5. The next thing to do is research your market and competitions.
6. Wait to receive inquiries from prospective buyers and communicate directly with potential customers on-site.
7. You can easily access the database of importers and exporters directly.
8. You now have access to and can buy trade leads database, if you want to.
9. You may now connect potential customers directly.
10. Network with companies in the B2B community.
11. Promote and market your business.

There are no Gold membership or Premium membership plans at Foreign Trade Online. **There is only one type of membership - FREE.**

According to Foreign Trade Online, "We believe every company around the world should have an equal opportunity to freely access the world market and promote their products or services without spending thousands of dollars on Gold or Premium membership."

When you become a member of Foreign Trade Online you can enjoy the following services for FREE:

1. Ability to post unlimited number of products.

2. You can send and receive unlimited inquiries from customers.

3. You are able to send and receive messages

4. You could set up your free company web site

5. Option to set up sub-accounts for your salesmen, if you have.

6. Liberty to send quotations to buyers who request them.

7. Provision to search the directory and contact importers directly

ECROBOT

http://www.ecrobot.com

ECROBOT has a **FREE** and **PREMIUM** membership plan. It is a South Korean B2B service provider.

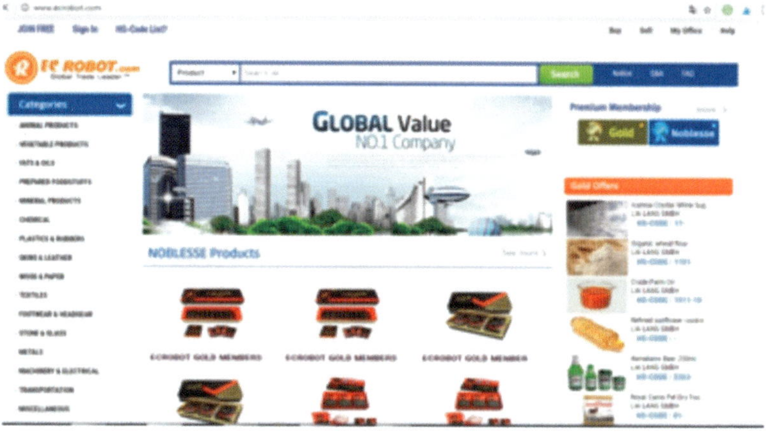

BusinessVibes

https://www.businessvibes.com/

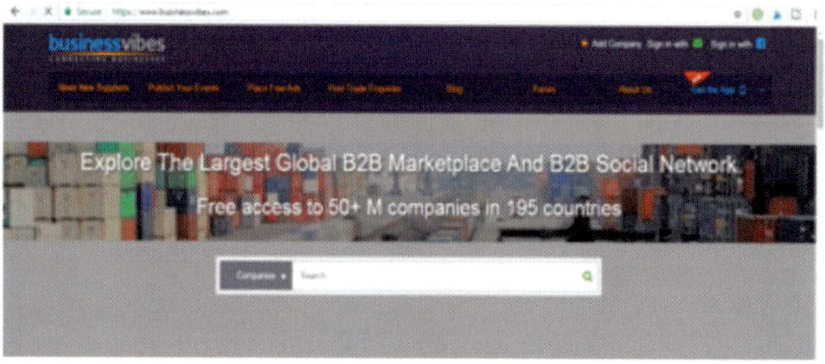

According to Business Vibes, meeting suppliers, manufacturers, Buyers and wholesalers has always been a difficult task for industrial professionals and business people. With the present growing economic environment, Businesses are looking for new and reliable techniques to contact other businesses either for selling, manufacturing or outsourcing services with highly competitive advantages. They always look for the best, which makes it even harder.

BusinessVibes present you the platform for business where you can easily meet and find verified **manufactures, buyers, suppliers**, and **marketing professionals** for **enhanced business relations**.

TRADEBOSS

http://www.tradeboss.com

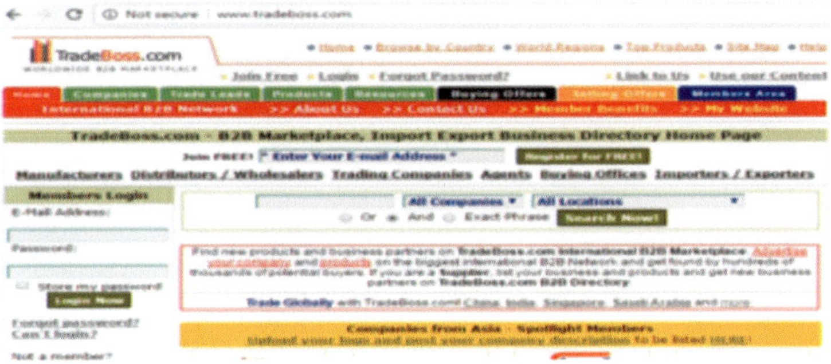

Find new products and business partners on TradeBoss.com, an international B2B e-Marketplace. Here you can advertise your products and company on the biggest international B2B Network and get found by hundreds of thousands of potential buyers from across different parts of the world.

For you who are Suppliers of products, you can list your business and products and get new business partners on TradeBoss.com B2B Directory.

I did a search for **bitter kola** on the website and found a number of African companies profiled.

EC PLAZA

http://www.ecplaza.net

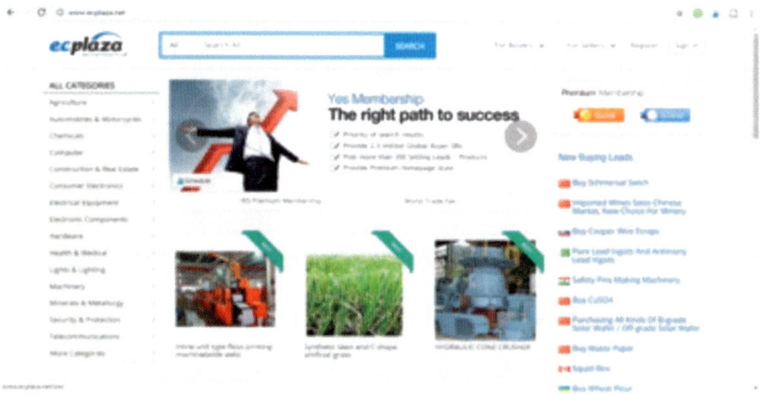

In 1996, EC Plaza started as a B2B business site which has now grown to No.1 Trade Leader providing online and offline services to well over 1,000,000 members. Apart from a B2B website, EC Plaza is also involved in offline trade-related services for small and medium enterprises (SMEs).

EC Plaza has a worldwide network and high brand recognition, they have extended their business field to the global market by providing great value such as cost saving, convenience and more business opportunities.

They have two categories of membership: free and premium (Silver and Gold packages)

EC21

http://www.ec21.com

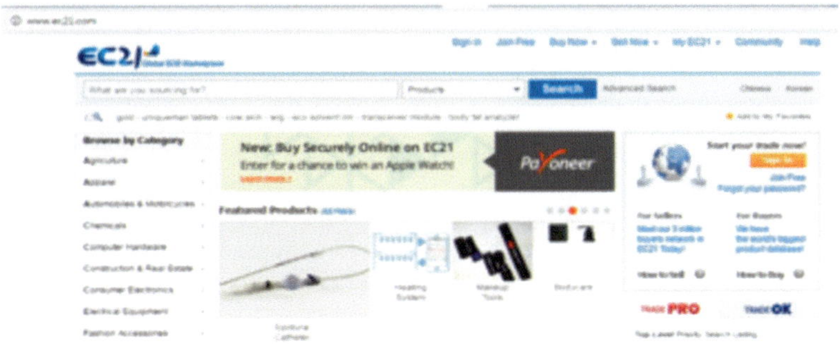

EC21.com has been facilitating global trade opportunities for small- and medium-sized enterprises (SMEs) for over twenty (20) years. EC21.com is one of the world's leading online B2B marketplaces; it is now connecting millions of suppliers and buyers worldwide. It has earned international recognition and trust in the global business community through its expertise in international trade and leading technology.

Currently EC21 has well over 7 million products, about 3.5 million buyers in its database, 2 million member companies and 3.5 million monthly new and repeat visitors. And it is still growing. It boasts of Business Information of **More than 3 Million Buyers from 245 Countries!**

They offer both FREE and PREMIUM services. Have a look at the membership plans below.

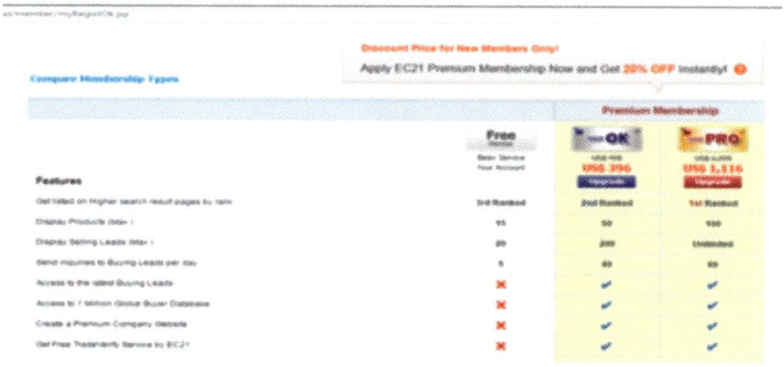

I did a search for **sesame seeds** buyers and found 219 prospects. See picture below:

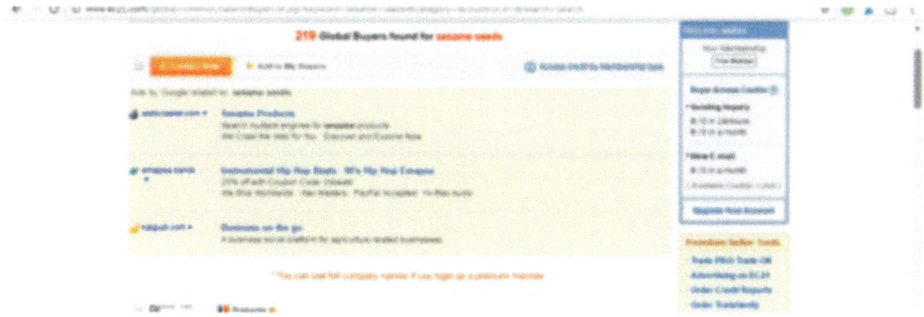

Global Suppliers Online

http://www.globalsuppliersonline.com

Global suppliers online is another B2B e-marketplace where you can get buyers of many export products. For instance I did a search for **Hibiscus Buyers** and found these results shown in the picture below. If you are looking to export **sesame**, **moringa** or just any other product, simply search and you will see Buyers of the product pop up for you.

EXPORTERS DOT SG

https://www.exporters.sg

A satisfied seller had this to say after using the services of Exporters dot sg:

"We have increased our sales by 30%, established many strong ties with buyers from over 5 continents."

The following are benefits of using Exporters.SG services:

- Exporters.SG helps you to find better trading partners in 600+ product categories from over 200 countries.
- Receive relevant buying leads and products offers, sell products, source products & more.
- Connect to thousands of members
- With over 500,000 business listings, you can network with businesses in your industry instantly.

Sign up a trial account - it's free!

They have both free and premium account. The premium account costs $59 per month.

To search for buying leads on Exporters.SG, choose BUYING LEADS, type the product you intend to get export leads for and click search.

See example below:

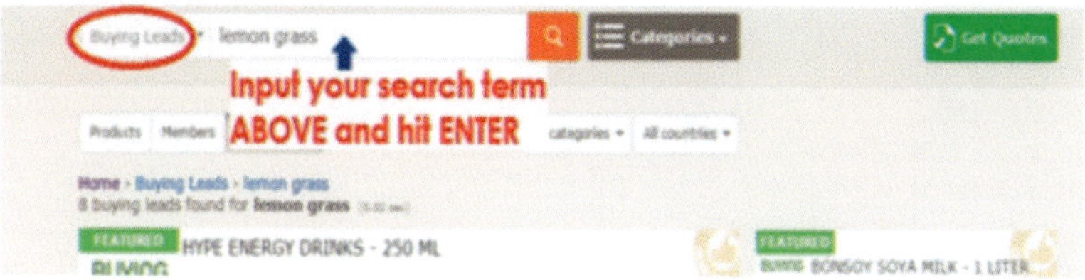

MORE B2B E-MARKETPLACES

For some of the following B2B e-marketplaces, you have to register and profile your company and products so buyers searching for your product can contact you. For others, you can search for buyers (importers) of your product and contact them directly for possible business.

E-MARKETPLACE	URL	LISTING
EXPORTAMERICA	www.ExportTradingNetwork.com	Premium
ALIBABA	www.alibaba.com	Free/ Premium
ECEUROPE	www.eceurope.com	Free
TOBOC	http://www.toboc.com	Free Forever
ALLPRODUCTS	www.allproducts.com	Free/ Premium
COMMERCE	www.commerce.com.tw	Free/ Premium
ECPLAZA	http://www.ecplaza.net/	Free/ Premium
EXPORTIMPOR	http://www.exportimp	Free

TSTRATEGIES	ortstrategies.com/	
TRADEFORD	http://www.tradeford.com/	FREE
TRADEKEY	http://www.tradekey.com/	Free/ Premium
EXPORTBUREAU	http://www.exportbureau.com/	Free/ Premium
TRADEINDIA	http:www.tradeindia.com	FREE
SELL147	http:www.sell147.com	FREE
EXPORTHONGKONG	http:www.exporthongkong.com	PAID ONLY
GLOBALSUPPLIERS	http:www.globalsuppliersonline.com	Free/ Premium
1STWORLDTRADEPORTAL	http://www.1stworldtradeportal.com/	Free
IMPORTEXPORTPLATFORM	http://www.importexportplatform.com	Free
KOMPASS	http://www.kompass.com	PAID
GLOBALMARKET	http://www.globalmarket.com/	FREE

TOOCLE	http://www.toocle.com/	Free
TOPTENWHOLESALE	http://www.toptenwholesale.com/	Free
BUSYTRADE	http://www.busytrade.com/	Free
ESOURCES	https://www.esources.co.uk	Free/Premium
DIYTRADE	http://www.diytrade.com/	**Free website**
INFOBANC	http://www.infobanc.com/	**Paid**
EXPORTERSINDIA	http://www.exportersindia.com	FREE
FIEO	https://www.fieo.org	FREE
EWORLDTRADEFAIR	http://www.eworldtradefair.com	FREE
SELLPRODUCTS	http://www.sellproducts.globalsources.com	Free/ Paid
DUBAIEXPORTERS	http://dubaiexporters.com	Free Listing
TRADERSCITY	http://www.traderscity	FREE

	.com/	
PANJIVA	https://panjiva.com	PREMI-UM
TRADOVE	https://www.tradove.com	Free
FOODDICTORIES	http://fooddirectories.com	Free/ Premium
EXPORT FO-RUM	http://www.export-forum.com/	Free/ Premium
ALLACTIONTRADE	http://www.allactiontrade.com/	Free/ Premium
MADEINCHINA	http://www.made-in-china.com/	Free/ Premium
BIZBILLA	http://www.bizbilla.com	Free/ Premium

CHAPTER FOUR

EXPORT PORTALS

What is an export portal?

An export portal may be defined as an online 'gateway' to export information, services and a network of people related to a particular topic. An export portal, therefore, is a website that provides visitors with a wide range of export-related information, services and people.

The main advantage of an export portal is that the portal owner has taken the effort to search out all the information that the user might possibly want to have access to and has put it together on a single, one-stop-shop website for convenience of the user.

Examples of export portals

The following are some export portals. Although each portal is designed differently, by spending a bit of time on each of these portals you will learn a lot.

PORTAL	URL	ORIGIN
ExportHelp	**http://www.exporthelp.co.za**	Africa
Austrade	http://www.austrade.gov.au/	Australia
Export61	http://www.export61.com.au/	Australia
Export.ca	http://www.export.ca/default.asp	Canada
Jetro	http://www.jetro.go.jp/	Japan
Nortrade	http://www.nortrade.com/	Norway
TDC	http://www.hktdc.com/	Hong Kong
International Enterprise Singapore	http://www.iesingapore.gov.sg/wps/portal	Singapore
Department of Export Promotion	http://www.thaitrade.com/	Thailand
Matrade	http://www.matrade.gov.my/	Malaysia
Irish Exporters' Association	http://www.matrade.gov.my/	Ireland
UK Trade and Investment	https://www.gov.uk/government/organisations/uk-trade-investment/	UK
Institute of Export	http://www.export.org.uk/	UK

Export.gov	http://www.export.gov/	US
TradePort	http://www.tradeport.org/	US
NZTE	http://www.nzte.govt.nz/	New Zealand
International Trade Administration	http://trade.gov/index.asp	US
ExportFocus	http://www.exportfocus.com/	US
EU Trade	http://ec.europa.eu/trade/index_en.htm	EU
Tradelink-eBiz	http://www.tradelink-ebiz.com/english/331n08or3m9a51l/index.html	Hong Kong
Austria Export	http://www.austria-export.biz/en/	Austria

CHAPTER FIVE

METHODS AND TOOLS FOR MAKING AND RECEIVING PAYMENT IN EXPORTING BUSINESS

In any export deal, the process of exporting is incomplete without receipt of payment by the Exporter. Export income is considered earned only when payment has been received. Below is the widely recognized means of payment in exporting:

Letter of Credit (L/C)

The Letter of Credit is the most popular and the safest method of payment for export businesses. It is an arrangement whereby the applicant (**the importer**) would request and instruct the Importer's bank or the issuing bank acting on his behalf, to pay **the exporter** the **bill of exchange** which is usually drawn by the beneficiary, or authorizes the advising/nominated bank to pay the beneficiary provided that the terms and conditions of the letter of credit are fully complied with.

Other methods of receiving payments include: Cash-in-Advance, Documentary Collections, etc.

CHAPTER SIX

GETTING EXPERT PROFESSIONAL SERVICES

If you are starting out for the first time in export business, it is highly recommended that you subscribe to the services of **Freight Forwarders** and/or other export business service providers.

This is important because, if you do not know the ropes of the business, some funny Importers might take advantage of your ignorance and cheat on you.

On no occasion should you export goods to anyone without first seeking advice from a freight forwarder.

Other processes of the export business are not covered in this book. So do yourself a favor to read about the entire export business to acquire adequate knowledge before venturing into it. This advice is for those just starting out in export business.

For you that have already gathered a lot of experience, I believe this book has helped you to get more export leads online and offline.

Kindly leave reviews for me.

CHAPTER SEVEN

KEY ONLINE EXPORTERS RESOURCES

AFRICAN GROWTH AND OPPORTUNITY ACT (AGOA)

If you are exporting from Africa, take advantage of this resource. **It is highly recommended.** Check it out...

https://agoa.info/

FREIGHT FORWARDERS DIRECTORY

Finding a reputable Freight forwarder is key to enhancing your export business. Look up the list and choose your country. Click the link below.

http://www.foreign-trade.com/freight-forwarders.htm

COMMODITY ONLINE

Get leads for many commodities here:

http://www.commodityonline.com

EXPORT ASSISTANCE

Export assistance is a non-profit organization that brings together experienced international business people who provide assistance and guidance in international markets. Check it out...

http://www.exportassistance.com

CBI

CBI is the Centre for the Promotion of Imports from **developing countries**

CBI helped Burke Agro and 23.478 entrepreneurs to become successful exporters on the European market. Learn more at

https://www.cbi.eu/

DUTY CALCULATOR

This resource helps you to compute duties on your export products.

https://www.dutycalculator.com

CHAPTER EIGHT

GLOBAL EXPORT STATISTICS

The following table shows the latest statistics surrounding the world's top exports. You will identify the products leading international sales as well as the most successful exporting countries as shown below.

Note that the product categories used are at the four-digit Harmonized Tariff System (HTS) code level in tariff manuals. This level of granularity should help readers spot trends and opportunities around the globe

World's Top Exports Report Card for Products

For your interest, below are the **TOP 20 export products** that attracted the highest dollar value in sales during the year 2015.

1. **Crude oil**: $786.3 billion (Down -50.3%)
2. **Cars**: $672.9 billion (Up 5.5%)
3. **Processed petroleum oils**: $605.9 bil lion (Down -36.5%)
4. **Phone system devices**: $532.2 billion (Up 34.7%)
5. **Integrated circuits assemblies**: $516.7 billion (Up 23.6%)
6. **Automobile parts/accessories**: $349.2 billion (Up 2.3%)
7. **Medication mixes in dosage**: $322.1 billion (Down -0.6%)
8. **Computers, optical readers**: $320.4 billion (Down -4.7%)
9. **Gold (unwrought):** $297.1 billion (Up 31.8%)
10. **Petroleum gases:** $250.2 billion (Down -39%)
11. **Blood fractions:**$127.6 billion (Up 41.9%)

12. **Aircraft, spacecraft:** $122.4 billion (Up 27.5%)
13. **Computer parts, accessories**: $121.3 billion (Down -9.4%)
14. **Diamonds (unmounted/unset):** $121.1 billion (Down -21.3%)
15. **Trucks**: $113.4 billion (Down -0.7%)
16. **Insulated wire/cable**: $112.4 billion (Up 7%)
17. **Solar power diodes**:$112 billion (Down -15.3%)
18. **Electro-medical equip**: $107.7 billion (Up 12.5%)
19. **Jewelry**: $97.7 billion (Up 18.4%)
20. **Printing machinery**: $93.8 billion (Down -20.3%).

Among the world's top 20 exports, the fastest-growing product from 2011 to 2015 was **blood fractions** including antisera with a 41.9% increase in value.

In second place were exported phone system devices including **smart phones**, up 34.7%. International sales of unrefined gold which appreciated by 31.8% over the 5-year period.

World's Top Exports Report Card for Countries

Below are the 20 countries that earned the highest total dollar amounts in export sales for the year 2015. Included within parenthesis is the indication to show whether the value of each country's exports increased or declined compared to 2011 metrics.

1. China: $2.282 trillion (Up 20.2%)
2. United States: $1.504 trillion (Up 1.5%)
3. Germany: $1.331 trillion (Down -10.2%)
4. Japan: $625 billion (Down -24.1%)
5. Netherlands: $567.7 billion (Down -15%)
6. South Korea: $526.9 billion (Down -5.1%)
7. France: $506.1 billion (Down -15.2%)
8. Hong Kong: $498.6 billion (Up 9.4%)
9. United Kingdom: $465.9 billion (Down -9.9%)

10. Italy: $458.8 billion (Down -12.3%)
11. Canada: $407.1 billion (Down -9.6%)
12. Belgium: $400.2 billion (Down -15.9%)
13. Mexico: $380.7 billion (Up 9%)
14. Singapore: $346.8 billion (Down -15.3%)
15. Russia: $333.5 billion (Down -35.5%)
16. Switzerland: $292 billion (Up 24.3%)
17. Taiwan: $280 billion (Down -9.4%)
18. Spain: $278.1 billion (Down -6.7%)
19. India: $264.4 billion (Down -12.3%)
20. Saudi Arabia: $213.4 billion (Down -40.4%).

Among the world's top 20 exporters, only five expanded the value of their exports since 2011: Switzerland (up 24.3%), China (up 20.2%), Hong Kong (up 9.4%), Mexico (up 9%) and the United States (up 1.5%).

Reflecting the downward spiral in oil prices, Saudi Arabia's exports dropped in value by -40.4% while Russian shipments devalued by -35.5% leading the declines for the top 20 global exporters. Japanese exports depreciated -24.1% while those Belgium fell -15.9% 2011 to 2015.

The above 20 countries shipped 73.3% of total exports during 2015.

List OF TOP TEN Global Export Products

Rank	Product Name	2015 Export Sales	Change 2011
1.	Crude oil	$786.3 billion	Down -50.3%
2.	Cars	$672.9 billion	Up 5.5%
3.	Processed petroleum oils	$605.9 billion	Down -36.5%
4.	Phone system devices	$532.2 billion	Up 34.7%
5.	Integrated circuits/micro assemblies	$516.7 billion	Up 23.6%
6.	Automobile parts/accessories	$349.2 billion	Up 2.3%
7.	Medication mixes in dosage	$322.1 billion	Down -0.6%
8.	Computers, optical readers	$320.4 billion	Down -4.7%
9.	Gold (unwrought)	$297.1 billion	Up 31.8%
10.	Petroleum gases	$250.2 billion	Down -39%

List of TOP TEN Exporting Countries

Rank	Country	2015 Export Sales	Change 2011
1.	China	$2.282 trillion	Up 20.2%
2.	United States	$1.504 trillion	Up 1.5%
3.	Germany	$1.331 trillion	Down -10.2%
4.	Japan	$625 billion	Down -24.1%
5.	Netherlands	$567.7 billion	Down -15%
6.	South Korea	$526.9 billion	Down -5.1%
7.	France	$506.1 billion	Down -15.2%
8.	Hong Kong	$498.6 billion	Up 9.4%
9.	United Kingdom	$465.9 billion	Down -9.9%
10.	Italy	$458.8 billion	Down -12.3%

Source: http://www.worldstopexports.com

Top Ten Exporting Countries In 2016 And Their Export Promotion Developments/ Councils Websites

SINGAPORE

https://www.iesingapore.gov.sg/

CHINA

http://www.ccpit.org.cn

USA

https://www.export.gov/

JAPAN

https://www.jetro.go.jp/en/

THAILAND

http://www.ditp.go.th

HONG KONG

https://www.tid.gov.hk/english/import_export/iemaincontent.html

INDIA

http://dgft.gov.in/

INDONESIA

http://djpen.kemendag.go.id/

AUSTRALIA

https://www.business.gov.au/info/run/import-and-export

VIET NAM

http://www.vietrade.gov.vn

CHAPTER NINE

EXPORTATION FORUMS

It is good to relate with other Exporters online. The following are exportation fora(forums) which you can join and relate with Exporters from other parts of the world. You could find export leads in these forums too. Endeavour to engage with the other users in the process of adding value to them by way of answering questions you have knowledge on.

In your bio, include your telephone and email contacts for easy communication. As you answer questions, be deliberate to mention that you can also supply your export products to interested parties.

Therefore visit the forum urls below, create accounts and contribute and/or search for possible export leads.

smallbusinessforums import-export

wholesaleforum.com import-export

thewholesaleforums.co.uk import-export

CHAPTER TEN

EXPORTATION FAQ

The following are some frequently asked questions on exportation.

What is an export license?

An export license is a government document that grants the Licensee the right to export commodities to other countries. If you are in the US, you can apply for an export license online at:

https://snapr.bis.doc.gov/snapr/.

Who is a freight forwarder?

The freight forwarder is an agent of the shipper—that is, the **cargo owner**, whether exporter or importer. The freight forwarder arranges transport and prepares documentation for the cargo.

What are 'Incoterms'?

INCOTERMS stand for **international commercial terms**. They are trade terms published by the **International Chamber of Commerce** (ICC) that are commonly used in both domestic and international trade business contracts. Usually, Incoterms are used to make international trade easier by helping business people from different countries to understand one another.

The ICC developed the Uniform Customs and Practice for Documentary Credits (UCP), Uniform Rules for Collection (URC), Incoterms, and other standards that facilitate worldwide trade.

What does the incoterm FOB mean?

FOB refers to Free on Board. The exporter has to load the goods on board the vessel specified by the importer. Cost and risk are shared between the seller and the buyer after the goods have been loaded on board the vessel. The seller must clear the goods for export. The term is applicable for maritime and inland waterway transport only but NOT for **multimodal sea**

transport in containers. There are various modes of transport: air, sea, rail, road, and parcel post. The use of more than one mode of transport is referred to as **multimodal transport**. The buyer must instruct the seller of the details of the vessel and the port where the goods are to be loaded, and there is no reference to, or provision for, the use of a carrier or forwarder. This is always used with the name of the shipment port; for example; FOB Lagos.

What does FCA mean in incoterms?

FCA which stands for "Free Carrier" means that the seller fulfils his responsibility to deliver when he has handed over the goods, cleared for export, into the hands of the carrier named by the buyer at the named location.

The seller pays for carriage to the named point of delivery, and the risk passes to the buyer when the goods are handed over to the first carrier. This is always used with the name of the place of delivery; for example, FCA Houston.

What is the meaning of DDP incoterm?

DDP stands for Delivered Duty Paid. It is a business transaction whereby the exporter pays for the entire prices related to transporting the merchandise and is absolutely liable for the products till they are received and transferred to the Importer.

It is a high risk transaction for the Exporter and is not advisable for new entrants into the market. It is more suitable for those who are established exporters with huge experience in the business.

So if you are just starting out in this business, I would advise you stick with a less risky agreement such as FOB.

What is incoterm ex works?

EXW stands for Ex Works. It is an incoterm that describes an agreement wherein the Exporter makes goods prepared for pickup at his or her factory or warehouse. The Importer takes responsibility for every other cost and risk from that point forward.

What is FAS in Incoterms?

FAS stands for Free Alongside Ship which means that the Exporter fulfils his obligation to deliver when the products have been put alongside the vessel at the named port of shipment. This implies that the Importer must take responsibility of all the costs and bear any risk of loss of or damage to the goods from that moment.

What does CPT mean in Incoterms?

CPT stands for Carriage Paid To. Here, the seller agrees to pay for carriage. Immediately after handing the goods over to the first carrier, the risk is transferred from the seller to the buyer. This is always used with the name of the destination; for example, CPT New York.

What does DAT mean in Incoterms?

DAT stands for Delivered at Terminal. In this agreement, the seller agrees to pay for carriage of their goods up to the port of destination and assumes all risks up to that point that where the goods are finally unloaded at the terminal, **excluding the costs that are related to import clearance**. This is always used with the name of the destination terminal; for example, DAT Port Elizabeth Beach Container Terminal Y

What is a trade mission?

A trade mission is an international trip by government authorities and agents that is organized by organizations of national governments for the sole purpose of looking out for global business openings in different nations.

Incoterms are updated from time to time; for instance, as of 2010, there were 11 rules, down from13 in the previous years.

Incoterms should be used in a way that all parties involved we know without any form of ambiguity, what is included in the price quoted and what is not. For instance, an exporter quotes US$10,000 EXW which means the Importer will take responsibility for the goods from the originating factory/warehouse of the Importer.

On the other hand, the signed contract stipulates US$10,000 DDP (instead of EXW) to New York. In this case, the exporter will have to pay freight costs and will be responsible for all export and import paperwork and payment of import duties. Why? Simply because instead of EXW, the signed contract spelt DDP. Mistakes like this make the difference between profit and loss in export business and call for absolute carefulness when signing contracts.

CONCLUSION

The most critical aspect of any business is **getting leads** as international business revolves around leads. Getting leads for import/export business is therefore a very essential aspect of your business.

E-market places and B2B/B2C websites are a great place to get potential export leads. Many import export businesses resort to these websites to get their export leads. Apart from that, it is highly important to have a professionally designed website to showcase your export products.

Offline marketing activities also complement your online efforts. Attending trade fairs enables you to network with other Exporters and also helps you to reach out to more potential buyers.

Overall, since the world is a global village, it is now easier to connect people from all over the world who will turn out to become your clients. The use of smart phones and other gadgets has really helped to make the world to be accessible right in your palms.

ABOUT THE AUTHOR

I am Solomon Ternder, happily married to my beautiful wife, OluDamilola. We are blessed with two kids: our precious Jewel-Mimi (Deem Deem), our daughter and the great man, Joe T.

I am an **Evangelist**, **Digital Marketing Consultant**, **Author**, **Researcher**, **Life Coach** and **Blogger**. I Blog at www.solomonternder.com
and www.moringawealthandhealth.com,

Together, my wife and I have passion for delivery of highly benefiting information through seminars, workshops, trainings and coaching.

You may reach us on solomonternder@gmail.com

Follow us on :

FB: https://web.facebook.com/solomonterndder

Twitter: https://twitter.com/wakesterndder

Mobile: +2348065387819

OTHER BOOKS BY THE AUTHOR

I have written the following amazing books. Kindly check them out too.

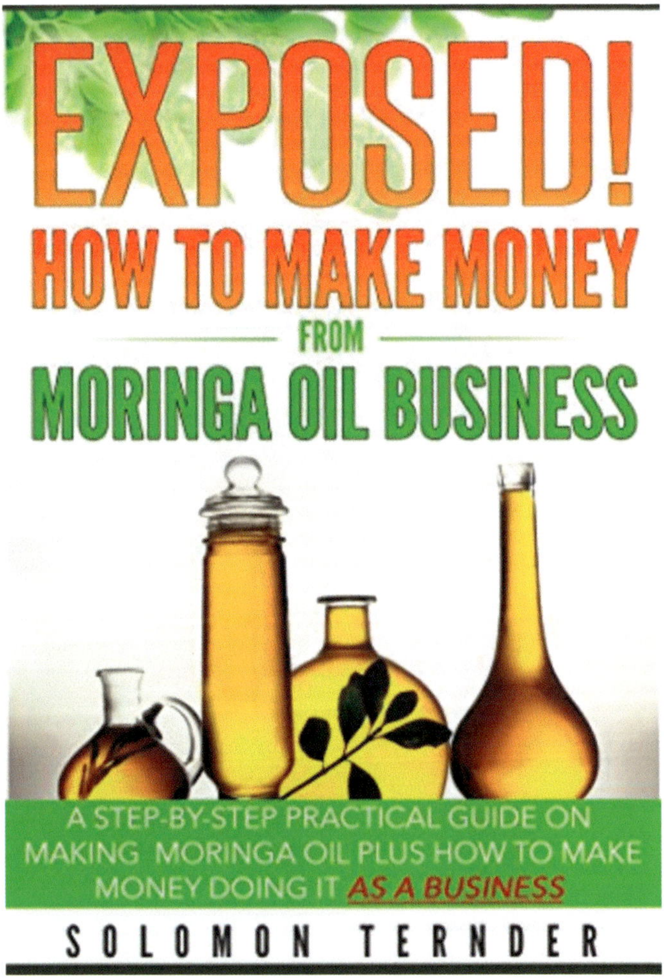

http://amzn.to/2pNiUPc

https://gumroad.com/l/LdFOP

Can I Ask A Favor?

If you enjoyed this book, found it useful or otherwise then I'd really appreciate it if you would write a short review and mail to solomonternder@gmail.com. I do read all the reviews personally so that I can continually write what people are wanting.

Thanks for your huge support! One moment please...

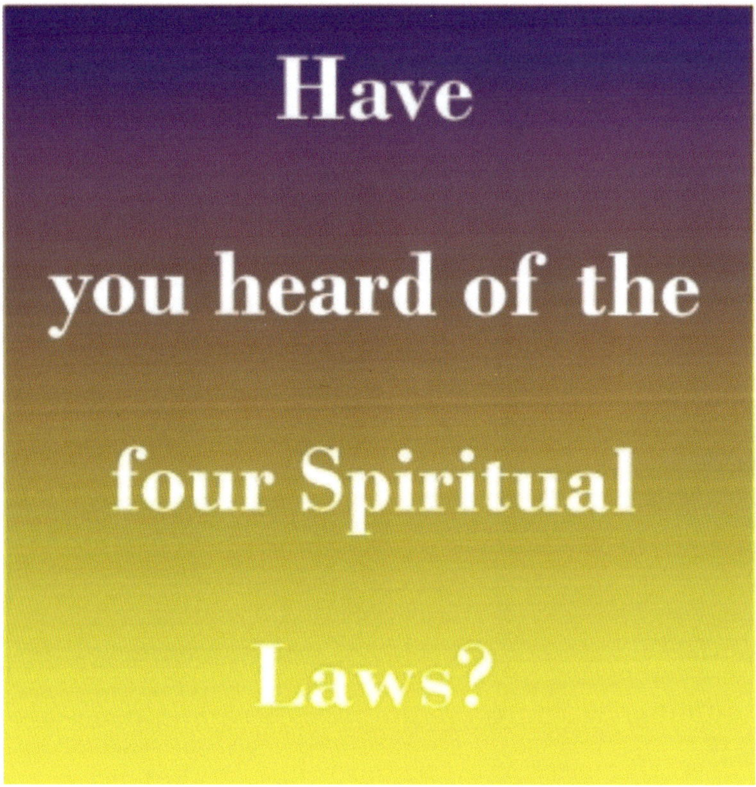

Check it out at www.4laws.com

25156352R00052

Printed in Great Britain
by Amazon